RELIGION AND SOCIETY:
EMERGING QUESTIONS
Monsignor W. Onclin Chair 2005

KATHOLIEKE UNIVERSITEIT LEUVEN
Faculteit Kerkelijk Recht
Faculty of Canon Law

RELIGION AND SOCIETY: EMERGING QUESTIONS

Monsignor W. Onclin Chair 2005

UITGEVERIJ PEETERS
LEUVEN
2005

ISBN 90-429-1630-3
D.2005/0602/66

INHOUDSTAFEL / TABLE OF CONTENTS

(NO) SEPARATION BETWEEN CHURCH AND STATE

RIK TORFS

INTRODUCTION

In the aftermath of September 11th, 2001, and in close connection with integration problems of certain categories of Muslims in western democracies, the notion of *separation between church and state* tends to become very popular again. *Again*, as separation as a notion had been thoroughly developed in various ways during the nineteenth century. In those days, church and state were competing for gaining control over life in society, over citizens and their activities. Key questions included the regulation of marriage, or the role the clergy can play in the public sphere. Separation in the nineteenth century was the opposite of what the notion at first glance may suggest. Without interaction, without rivalry, no one would ever have invented such an apparently radical notion as *separation*. Ongoing interaction gave shape to the notion of separation, meant to regulate the latter. Today, after a long period of silence, separation between church and state emerges again in the public discussion. What does this unexpected reappearance really mean? Could it be that the strong connection between church and state once inspiring the birth of the notion of separation, emerges again?

In this brief reflection, I will analyse this question in three different centuries, namely the nineteenth in which the notion of separation was given shape; the twentieth century during which it surprisingly lost momentum; and finally this century, offering dramatically new perspectives.

SEPARATION IN THE NINETEENTH CENTURY

Separation in the nineteenth century is the legal translation of what one could commonly call *rivalry*. The nineteenth century happened to be the period during which the nation-state steadily developed. It was also the era in which the church needed to assert itself, and in certain countries, tried to recover from the devastating consequences caused by the French Revolution. A new equilibrium had to be reached. Both the church and the state experienced the need to develop a credible strategy. In that regard, an element of paramount importance was their position vis-à-vis their traditional rival. Consequently, relationships between church and state became a dominant political issue.

When two strong competitors are present, *separation* can be a key notion in preserving the dignity of both. As a matter of fact, that is what happened in the first six or seven decades of the century, when separation did not entail negative consequences for either of the two main players.

At the beginning of the century, the French philosopher Lamennais advocated a separation between church and state for the sake of the church. By being liberated of political concerns, the church could focus on its spiritual mission and could safeguard the purity that it should always foster. Separation, in that perspective, came close to liberation. The church was freed from a burden; it was no longer obliged to fulfil a political and administrative role that was deep-rooted in history, although without being strictly connected with the original religious message.

Several decades later, separation as a concept became more balanced. Its purpose was not any longer to preserve the church from earthly concerns. Gradually, true liberalism became the underlying motivation for fostering a real separation between church and state. This idea is expressed in a very clear way by the maxim used by Cavour, *Libera chiesa in libero stato*. Here, the binding factor is liberty. Certainly, both the church and the state enjoy its benefits. And yet, it is liberty what is truly aimed at, and not the good of the church, nor the prospering of the state.

It was some years later, near the end of the century, that separation became in a more outspoken way a notion *hostile* to the church. In countries where the entanglement between both institutions remained unchanged, the need for new solutions led gradually to more radical political initiatives aiming at a separation at any price, including the loss of the position and privileges that in many countries the church had always enjoyed.

To sum up, the trend that we can discern during the nineteenth century shows two things. On the one hand, the notion of separation remains present throughout the century. On the other hand, its content varies, starting from a positive attitude vis-à-vis the church (Lamennais), via a balanced position just fostering liberty (Cavour), to an urgent claim for separation, if necessary at the expense of the church. But then again, separation cannot be understood without a huge number of contacts, without rivalry, without intimate connections between both major players of nineteenth century Europe.

Certainly, both church and state used the term *separation* in order to improve their own legal and social position, and yet, they never were entirely consistent in implementing separation in their own policy. Some examples clearly illustrate this point.

The Roman Catholic church defined itself as a *societas perfecta,* a perfect society. Perfection, of course, has no moral connotations, it simply underscores the self-sufficient character of the church as an institution. The church functions autonomously, relying upon a proper legal system, making use of financial and other material assets, and thus independent of any mandatory external support. But then again, the notion of the perfect society culminated at the very moment that the papal states disintegrated as a result of the unification of Italy. Without this loss of territory, the perfect society would have appeared to be less urgent. Moreover, the notion of perfect society remained one-sided. Whereas the church claimed its autonomy and its independence, most of the time it did not refuse moral, ceremonial and financial state support. In that regard, separation never was complete true separation. It came closer to the idea of *church autonomy*, yet an autonomy without refusing presents from the traditional rival. Obviously, a separation with presents never can be a true and radical separation.

A similar attitude can be discerned at the level of the state. The newly constructed nation-state badly needed full independence from clerical influences. Yet at the same time, it was not prepared to acknowledge church activity as irrelevant in the public sphere. Consequently, separation remained a relative notion. In many European countries, no religious marriage was possible without a previously concluded civil one. This is an obvious denial of full separation. Of course, the exception is understandable, as the control on marriage was an important element in the struggle for control over the population in general.

In other words, separation in the nineteenth century was important in order to guarantee *mutual independence* of both players. The pressing need for mutual independence means that the risk of dependence was not just virtual. Moreover, mutual independence was *exactly* what both competitors eventually achieved. They often called the system a system of separation, as this notion contains some radical elegance. Yet, the purity that the term suggests, clearly remained absent.

SEPARATION IN THE TWENTIETH CENTURY

During the twentieth century, the notion of separation started living a life on its own. Not so much, of course, in countries with a concordatarian tradition, where mutual agreement between church and state remained the central notion of the system. Yet in the meantime, more in general, separation became an almost *petrified term* describing the relationships between church and state. Gradually, their mutual rivalry evaporated. Slowly, *separation* as a notion characterising their relationship became commonly used. For no real discussion emerged, separation as the key term characterising relationships between church and state became more or less unchallenged. The notion survived, the underlying struggle evaporated.

After World War I, and more drastically so after World War II, key questions in European society became subject to a paradigm shift. The main problems in society were no longer the position of the church or the mutual relationship between the two fierce competitors of the nineteenth century. What really counted was the elaboration of democracy, the protection of the rule of law, and, somewhat later, after World War II, the construction of the welfare state. Especially in the late forties of the last century, after the disasters caused by the war, church and state gradually became partners instead of rivals. They no longer tried to gain control over the people; they both collaborated in order to create a welfare state including both better standards of living and appealing spiritual values. The combination of material wealth and immaterial ideas were the best guarantee against totalitarianism and dictatorial regimes.

A peculiar consequence of this evolution is that separation tended to become stricter at a moment that separation was no longer a political issue of high importance. That phenomenon may be typical of history: one only gets what he wants when he is no longer interested in obtaining it. Separation in the twentieth century became purer than in the previous era, not as a result of a deliberate policy, but as a consequence of the lack of any new policy whatsoever with regard to church and state relationships. The state was no longer deeply interested in church marriages, even if it did not always abrogate nineteenth century measures trying to regulate them. Churches, from their side, no longer tried to obtain material advantages from the secular state, although, of course, they were not eager to abandon the privileges they had acquired before. The norms that already existed very often survived, yet most of the time the underlying reason for the maintenance of the old system was a *deep lack of interest* in changing a situation that in the eyes of many seemed to be petrified.

As a result of the *decreased rivalry*, the old notion of separation became more real than ever before. Yet, the *mental relationship* between both players lost momentum. To conclude, *separation* eventually won, at a moment that nobody was interested in victory anymore.

The newly achieved, (true) separation entailed some unexpected consequences. It led to a degree of politeness, which at times went too far. For instance, in many countries, sexual abuse committed by clergymen was very cautiously dealt with by secular tribunals. Judges were eager to avoid diplomatic incidents with the church and its leaders. They often facilitated an off the record, informal solution. In public debate, politicians often defined religion as a *private matter*. Obviously, from a certain perspective, they were right. In a democratic state, governed by the rule of law, it is everybody's personal choice to be religious or not. No external authority whatsoever has the right to interfere with this choice. In that regard, religion definitely is a private matter.

And yet, by defining religion as a private matter, politicians implicitly consider religion and religious adherence as irrelevant for politics and public life. Too often, *private* means *irrelevant*. By calling something private, the idea is nourished that the interest concerned is very personal, truly intimate, and, for that reason, needs special protection. What really matters, however, is not the protection of privacy, but the denial of any public relevance connected with religion. This is a common strategy: the strategy of *elimination by protection*. Until deep into the twentieth century, politicians in a secularised Western Europe could not even imagine religion being a driving force leading citizens to outspoken options in both politics and society.

To say it in another way, in the nineteenth century the notion of *separation* indicated the vulnerable equilibrium between church and state. It was a visit or calling card that very often just covered a less radical, but effective mutual independence. In the twentieth century, the same notion of separation became synonymous with political irrelevance. The notion remained and became even more radical, while the underlying tension completely disappeared.

SEPARATION IN THE TWENTY-FIRST CENTURY

In some regard, in this century, we come closer to the flavour of the nineteenth century again. As a result of the emergence of the multicultural society and the visible presence of Islam in the West, separation

becomes once more *a notion with a content*. Whereas during the twentieth century, few people used the notion separation because some form of
separation *really* existed, the term separation emerges again, more than
ever, in an era during which the content of separation clearly tends to
disappear.

Indeed, religion is back in town. Some people use it as a source of
inspiration for terrorism. Others invoke it in order to deny full citizen-
ship to Muslims. Whether one likes it or not, religion has become a
political issue again. Of course, one can try to make religion invisible by
prohibiting the wearing of headscarves. And one can try to minimise its
impact by loudly praising the numerous benefits of the secular state, of
laïcité. But then again, those relying upon separation know deep in their
heart that true separation is less possible than it was ever before. Such an
attitude can be compared to an *invocatio Dei* at a moment of disaster and
cataclysm, when God's absence (seemingly) eclipses his presence.

Although the verbal triumph of separation at the very moment of its
decline is understandable, we should not try to escape current political
problems. The latter implies the need for a real *religious policy* from the
side of the modern state. This policy should rest upon two pillars.

Firstly, religious freedom is the cornerstone of every further reflection. Democracy and the rule of law include everybody's freedom to
believe or not to believe, to be a member of a religious group or to
remain independent, to join a community of faith or to leave it. Moreover, religious groups have the right to organise themselves freely,
which implies the right to participate actively in legal and in public life.

Secondly, the legal and practical relationships between church and
state, that can only be given shape once full (though not limitless,
see art. 9 § 2 ECHR) religious liberty is granted to all, should be the
object of a lucidly elaborated public policy. Here, similarities with the
nineteenth century are obvious. For instance, perhaps one could use, in
that perspective, the regular, open and transparent dialogue that the
European constitution envisages between the Union and religious
groups. Something else is thinkable, namely the conclusion of contracts
and covenants between religious groups and states (or the European
Union) in case these religious groups freely cope with the standards of
modern democratic society, and do show some willingness to collabo-
rate in the further elaboration of a European style democratic welfare
state. In other words, the *lack of absolute separation* between church
and state could be used in order to strengthen the midfield in society. It
could also play a part in order to foster participative democracy as put

forward by the European constitution. Relationships between church and state can be a decisive factor in successfully elaborating a peaceful multicultural society. The required negotiation margin for doing so, that lacks on the basic level of religious freedom, can be developed without legal obstacles on the superior level of church and state relationships.

Just one example from my own country. In the intermediate report of the Belgian Commission for Intercultural Dialogue, state support for religious groups is defined as possibly dependent on the coping of the latter with the basic principles of democratic society and with human rights.

To put it bluntly once again, the notion of *separation* is back in town, because its complete implementation is more impossible than ever. Apparently, we need to make a choice between the *verbal notion* of separation (nineteenth and twenty-first century) and its *concrete existence* (twentieth century). We cannot have them both.

THE CANONS ON JURIDICAL ACTS APPLIED TO MARRIAGE

MICHAEL P. HILBERT, S.J.

1. INTRODUCTION

My purpose in this presentation is to present in a synthetic manner one general norm of canon law, the norm contained in canons 124-126 of the Code of Canon Law of 1983, the norm which expresses the nature of a juridical act, and then to place against that background the specific norms on marriage, which we find in canons 1055-1058. We will examine in what ways persons are capable (and incapable) of positing this particular juridical act, what are the constitutive elements, and finally which formalities are required for the validity of marriage. In this way I hope to bring into relief, as it were, the particularity of marriage in its juridical physiognomy. For the canonists present, this will be nothing new, although I hope it will prove to be a useful exercise in applying general norms to particular norms; for the non-canonists present, I will strive to be clear!

2. THE JURIDICAL ACT

In the Book on General Norms in the Code of Canon Law, we find first the canons on the person, physical and juridical, in Title VI. Immediately following, in Title VII, we find the norms on juridical acts, and the logic of such an ordering should be evident. The Church is the People of God, and the internal ordering of the relationships among the members of the Church, from this perspective, is based in large part on the appropriate, legitimate actions of the faithful. Thus, having identified who are persons in the Church, the legislation establishes what are the juridical acts performed by those persons, the essential elements that make the acts valid, the conditions under which the acts are to be considered legitimate, and the causes of an invalid, or null, act. Let us look at the first canon of Title VII:

Can. 124 - § 1. Ad validitatem actus iuridici requiritur ut a persona habili sit positus, atque in eodem adsint quae actum ipsum essentialiter constituunt, necnon sollemnia et requisita iure ad validitatem actus imposita.
§ 2. Actus iuridicus quoad sua elementa externa rite positus praesumitur validus.

The canon does not give a definition of juridical act (the law abhors definitions), but presents instead the essential elements for the validity of an act. We must refer to doctrine then to get a better idea of what we mean by a juridical act. The doctrine is canonical doctrine mostly, but it must be said that civil law doctrine does not differ substantially from the canonical doctrine, and even in some ways develops it further.

Robleda defines a juridical act as, "an externally manifested act of the will by which a certain juridical effect is intended." The features that distinguish the act are its voluntary nature, the fact that is deliberate, an act of the will, and that the effect of the action is intended. It must be externally manifested; an action that remains internal has no effect, no consequences for the life of the community or the relationships among persons.

We must distinguish, first of all, juridical acts from juridical facts. The law recognizes certain juridical effects for juridical facts. A juridical fact can be natural or human. Some examples of each. A natural juridical fact is an earthquake or a fire that begins naturally (not arson), some natural happening that nonetheless has juridical effects (the insurance company must pay). Birth and death are also natural juridical facts. A human juridical fact can be further distinguished in voluntary and non voluntary facts. A non voluntary human fact is, for example, the administration of the sacrament of baptism which automatically has as one of its effects the registration of the baptised person into a particular ritual church or ecclesial communion, even though this particular effect was in no way intended. Another example is the automatic acquisition of quasi-domicile in the parish where one lives for three months (can. 102, §2), again even if this particular juridical effect was not intended. Finally, we have the voluntary human juridical fact, which, due to the very element of the will ("voluntary") is equivalent to the juridical act. For example, the signing of a contract, an administrative decree, the renouncing of an office, insofar as they are human, voluntary acts intended to have certain juridical effects, they are juridical acts in the strict sense.

Our canon then deals with both private and public juridical acts and puts forth the essential elements for their validity. The following canons establish those defects which can cause the inexistence, the invalidity, or the possibility of rescinding the act. Let us look now at the essential elements. There are three conditions which are required for the validity of the act: the capacity of the person to act, the constitutive elements of the act itself, and the formalities required by law for the validity of the act.

3. THE CAPACITY OF THE PERSON

As regards the capacity or ability to act, the doctrine speaks of natural capacity, general or canonical capacity, specific capacity, and competence. Natural capacity is, *ex iure naturae*, the capacity to intend something, the human freedom and awareness that are necessary for any human act. The general juridical capacity to act signifies that the person is the subject of rights and obligations in the Church, and has the required age and responsibility. An infant, while a person and subject of rights, has not the general capacity to act. The specific capacity refers to the act to be placed and signifies that the person is able to, and is not impeded, from the placing of the act. For example, according to canon 1024, only a baptised male can receive the sacrament of Orders: *Sacram ordinationem valide recipit solus vir baptizatus.*

To make our first application to marriage of this general norm, we turn to canon 1057 §1:

> Can. 1057 - § 1. Matrimonium facit partium consensus inter personas iure habiles legitime manifestatus, qui nulla humana potestate suppleri valet.

Here we address the phrase "iure habiles." This canon always has to be read, in my opinion, together with the very next canon, 1058: "Omnes possunt matrimonium contrahere, qui iure non prohibentur." The "ius connubii" is one of the fundamental rights of the human person, but it is not an absolute right. Being an institution not merely private but essentially social, marriage can and must be regulated by norms that protect the common good of society. Only those who are juridically capable can validly posit this particular juridical act of marriage (the capacity that we call competence will be seen below, when we speak of the formalities required by law). That is to say, to use the terminology of the doctrine contained in the general norm they must be naturally, canonically, and specifically able, whether it be for any marriage or this particular marriage. We can offer some examples of each type of capacity, or rather incapacity, which are found in the diriment impediments. According to canon 1073, "Impedimentum dirimens personam inhabilem reddit ad matrimonium valide contrahendum." The commentary

"The Canon Law: Letter and Spirit" explains concisely: "It is an objective circumstance attaching to a person which, in virtue of either divine or human law, makes that person incapable of validly contracting marriage – whether with anyone...or with a certain person" (p. 589).

To begin with the most simple category, the specific incapacity to marry a specific person arising from a diriment impediment, we have, for example, the impediment of disparity of cult (c.1086), the impediment of abduction (c. 1089), the impediment of crime (c. 1090), the impediment of consanguinity (c. 1091), the impediment of affinity (c. 1092), the impediment of public propriety (c. 1093), and the impediment of legal adoption (c. 1094). These are all impediments of positive ecclesiastical law, in the interests of the spouses, the family, and the common good of society. They render the spouse incapable of entering this particular marriage with this specific person, and thus they fall into the category of specific capability.

The next more general category, the canonical "habilitas," encompasses impediments arising from either divine positive law or positive ecclesiastical law, and that render the person incapable of marrying anyone. For example, the impediment of non-age (c. 1083), is of positive ecclesiastical law and determines the minimum age below which a person cannot validly marry (we will see below what natural law requires in this regard); the impediment of the bond of a previous marriage (c. 1085), arises from natural law as well as positive divine law, based on the essential properties of marriage, indissolubility and especially unity, and as such can be counted among the natural incapacities; the impediment of sacred orders (c. 1087), related of course to the law of celibacy in the Latin Church, a tradition dating back to the 4th century; the impediment of public perpetual vow of chastity (c. 1088), again an ecclesiastical law that safeguards a precious ethical-religious value in the church.

Finally, there is one impedimentum dirimens that, according to the prevalent doctrine, arises from natural law, the impediment of impotence (c. 1084). The canon reads thus:

> Can. 1084 - § 1. Impotentia coeundi antecedens et perpetua, sive ex parte viri sive ex parte mulieris, sive absoluta sive relativa, matrimonium ex ipsa eius natura dirimit.
> § 2. Si impedimentum impotentiae dubium sit, sive dubio iuris sive dubio facti, matrimonium non est impediendum nec, stante dubio, nullum declarandum.
> § 3. Sterilitas matrimonium nec prohibet nec dirimit, firmo praescripto can. 1098.

Note the phrase, "Ex ipsa eius natura." The Code of Canon Law of 1917 used the expression "ipso naturae iure" (c. 1086 § 1 CIC/17), but despite the change in wording the doctrine is firm, and the impediment involves the antecedent, perpetual, and certain inability to have sexual intercourse. Thus, going back to the categories provided by our general norm, we have here an example of a natural inability.

To summarize, we saw that the doctrine speaks of natural, canonical, and specific juridical capability of a person to posit a juridical act. We then applied the various impediments to marriage to these categories in order to distinguish the nature of each impediment. Two of the impediments, previous bond of marriage and impotence, involve the very nature of marriage; the others, arising from positive divine law and/or ecclesiastical law, constitute canonical and specific, but not natural capability. Now let us look at the next phrase of canon 124.

4. THE CONSTITUTIVE ELEMENTS

"...atque in eodem adsint quae actum ipsum essentialiter constituunt." Together with the capacity of the acting person, the juridical act must have those constitutive elements, without which the act is null. Here we address, first and foremost, the will of the acting person, and second, the specific elements that constitute marriage.

Recall the definition of juridical act offered by Robleda: an act of the will by which a certain juridical effect is intended. Canons 125 and 126 establish those constraints on the intellect and the will which render the act invalid, and in some cases non-existent. Such constraints block or compromise the voluntary aspect of the act, and as we have seen it is the voluntary aspect that renders the act a human act. The canons read as follows:

> Can. 125 - § 1. Actus positus ex vi ab extrinseco personae illata, cui ipsa nequaquam resistere potuit, pro infecto habetur.
> § 2. Actus positus ex metu gravi, iniuste incusso, aut ex dolo, valet, nisi aliud iure caveatur; sed potest per sententiam iudicis rescindi, sive ad instantiam partis laesae eiusve in iure successorum sive ex officio.
> Can. 126 - Actus positus ex ignorantia aut ex errore, qui versetur circa id quod eius substantiam constituit, aut qui recidit in condicionem *sine qua non*, irritus est; secus valet, nisi aliud iure caveatur, sed actus ex ignorantia aut ex errore initus locum dare potest actioni rescissoriae ad normam iuris.

The will of the person can be affected negatively by force and fear, the intellect by deceit, ignorance and error. The doctrine also makes the distinction between extrinsic factors – force, fear, and deceit – and intrinsic factors – ignorance and error. A brief word on each.

"Force" signifies a physical violence imposed from the outside, unable to be resisted. As a consequence of this force, the freedom of the person is entirely absent and the act "pro infecto habetur" – not simply null, inexistent. Besides the specific norm on marriage, which we will see below, the Code of Canon Law expressly stipulates other acts rendered null by force: religious profession (c. 656), judicial confession of the parties in a trial (c. 1538), and a judicial sentence (c. 1620, 3°), among others.

"Fear" is also called "moral force" and "a psychological pressure through threats." As the canon states, the effect of fear, even if it is grave and unjustly inflicted, on the will of the person is not such that the act is null, unless the law provides otherwise. The freedom of the person is diminished but not entirely taken away, that is the general norm. The law does provide otherwise in certain cases, including marriage, as we will see.

"Deceit" ("dolus"), as it is used here with regard to juridical acts, signifies those tricks and lies and subterfuge used to lead the person into error, to make the person do something that otherwise he would not do. As we saw above, it is considered in the doctrine as an extrinsic factor which influences the intellect. The will freely chooses but it has been tricked by falsehoods. For this reason the general norm is that the act is valid. If, however, the deceit is such that it leads to error concerning the substance of the act, or leads to a condition *sine qua non*, as canon 126 states, the act is null. For both fear and deceit, while the acts per se are valid, they can be rescinded by a court judgment, according to § 2 of canon 125. As we will see, however, this possibility is not applicable to a marriage declared null due to fear or deceit, which is an entirely different juridical reality.

"Ignorance" and "error" are commonly described, respectively, as "lack of sufficient knowledge" and "false judgment." Canon 126 echoes canon 124 when it determines the nullity of an act due to ignorance or error "which concerns the substance of the act" – "circa id quod eius substantiam constituit." When the constitutive elements of an act are vitiated by ignorance or error, the act is null; otherwise, if the ignorance or error is merely accidental, the act remains valid, but can be rescinded, as with fear and deceit.

Having studied the general norm regarding the constitutive element of the juridical act which is the will of the acting person, and having enumerated the conditions and causes for the diminishment and removal of that essential element, we can now consider the constitutive elements of marriage and see how the general norms can be applied to them.

The first relevant canon is 1057, seen above. We now put our attention to the beginning phrase of the canon: "§1. Matrimonium facit partium consensus." This phrase descends directly from Roman Law, in Ulpianus' words, "Nuptias consensus facit." Whereas for any juridical act the free consent of the will is a necessary element, a required feature, in marriage it is a constitutive element. The consent which brings into being a marriage is not just one of the requirements for the validity of the act, it is that which "essentialiter" constitutes the act! It has been called "the genetic cause of marriage," and "intrinsically sufficient." In other types of juridical acts, the constitutive elements are different. For example, the water in baptism, or the parties to and the object of a contract. In these cases, the consent is an essential though generic element, but the nature of those juridical acts determines other constitutive elements. In marriage, the consent is both the generic and the specific, constitutive, "genetic," element, and thus we must be clear on the object of the consent and then see how a defect in consent in marriage takes on a particularly significant normative importance.

In identifying the object of marital consent, let us look at §2 of canon 1057:

> Consensus matrimonialis est actus voluntatis, quo vir et mulier foedere irrevocabili sese mutuo tradunt et accipiunt ad constituendum matrimonium.

The object of the consent is the mutual giving and accepting of a man and a woman in an irrevocable covenant for the purpose of establishing a marriage, that is, that partnership of their whole life – "totius vitae consortium" in the words of canon 1055 §1, "intima communitas vitae et amoris coniugalis" in the words of the Second Vatican Council (GS 48,1). And in canons 1055 §1 and 1066, we find the ends of marriage and its essential properties: the wellbeing of the spouses and the procreation and education of offspring; unity and indissolubility.

Given the fact that consent is constitutive element of marriage, it is not surprising that the particular norms regulating this consent form a major chapter in the title on marriage in the code. Some pertinent observations must be made regarding these norms, especially in light of the foregoing discussion on the capacity of the person to posit juridical acts and the causes and conditions whereby the act itself is null.

We affirmed that the doctrine speaks of natural capacity, that is, *ex iure naturae*, the capacity to intend something, the human freedom and awareness that are necessary for any human act. The first canon in the chapter on marriage consent, canon 1095, addresses this incapacity in three numbers, three figures of a natural incapacity, due to: 1° lack of sufficient use of reason; 2° grave defect in discretion of judgment concerning the essential matrimonial rights and obligations to be mutually given and accepted; and 3° the inability to assume the essential obligations of marriage because of causes of a psychological nature. Without going into the extensive doctrinal and jurisprudential discussion concerning this canon, as we apply this norm to the general norm on juridical acts we see that it is a natural incapacity.

The following canons, on the other hand, find their place among the constitutive elements of the juridical act, the will of the acting person. We saw how force and fear, deceit and ignorance and error can render a juridical act null, as a general norm. As we study the particular norms on marriage consent, we note the following important differences:

A. Canon 1103 addresses the question of force and fear. As to force, the norm is totally in line with c. 125 – the marriage is null "ipso naturae iure." As to fear, however, recall that the general norm permits the rescinding of the act which is otherwise valid. The essential property of marriage which is its indissolubility does not allow the application of the general norm in this case, and the marriage can be declared null if the fear is grave, imposed from without, and from which the person has no escape other than choosing marriage. Thus we have a case where, as canon 125 permits, the law "provides otherwise." This is a determination of ecclesiastical, not natural, law.

B. With regard to deceit, the general norm does not attribute invalidating force unless the deceit, in the words of canon 126, leads to an error concerning the substance of the act. The corresponding particular norm for marriage is found in canon 1098:

> Qui matrimonium init deceptus dolo, ad obtinendum consensum patrato, circa aliquam alterius partis qualitatem, quae suapte natura consortium vitae coniugalis graviter perturbare potest, invalide contrahit.

This positive law, again taking into account that the nature of marriage does not allow for the rescinding of the act, establishes the conditions under which the marriage consent can be declared defective and the marriage null: the deceit must be direct ("ad obtinendum consensum"), that it concerns some quality of the other person (not third parties), and that it can seriously disrupt the partnership of conjugal life. Here, too, we have a case where the particular norm derogates from the general norm.

C. Finally, concerning ignorance and error, the canons on marriage consent specify the minimum due knowledge required for marriage – "that marriage is a permanent partnership between a man and a woman, ordered to the procreation of children through some form of sexual cooperation" (c. 1096 §1) – and legislate for the various kinds of error that are possible in marriage: error of person invalidates the marriage (c. 1097 §1), error about a quality of the person directly and principally intended invalidates the marriage (c. 1097 §2), error caused by deceit as seen above (c. 1098), error concerning the law of marriage does not vitiate the consent provided it does not determine the will (c. 1099). All of these norms are in harmony with the general norm, i.e., that ignorance and error do not render the juridical act null unless they touch on the very substance of the act.

5. THE FORMALITIES AND REQUIREMENTS

The third and final aspect of the general norm concerning the validity of juridical acts is found in the phrase "necnon solemnia et requisite iure ad validitatem actus imposita." The corresponding phrase in canon 1057 §1 is "legitime manifestatus."

One might ask why "mere" formalities should be considered to affect the validity of a juridical act, when the more substantial factors – the capacity of the person and the constitutive elements of the act itself – would seem to suffice in assuring the good order of the community and the correct regulation of relationships between persons. This is somewhat confirmed by the second paragraph of canon 124: "§2. Actus iuridicus quoad sua elementa externa rite positus praesumitur validus." This presumption of validity is "iuris tantum" and this allows contrary proof. The general norm wants to protect certain juridical acts of particular importance, such as documents of the local Ordinary (c. 474), and marriage. It thus leaves to the various particular norms the possibility of imposing formalities and other requirements for the validity of the act.

In the canons on marriage, I can briefly point out one example of a formality and one example of a requirement, both established with the force of invalidating the act in the case of their non-observance.

The formality is of course the canonical form, including the norms for the declaration of the consent of the parties, the presence of two witnesses, those who may validly – either through ordinary or delegated power – assist at the celebration and receive the consent of the spouses.

The canonical form of marriage has a long and interesting history, and the norms are rather extensive and do permit some exceptions. However, the formalities imposed "ad validitatem" are those listed above, and they are found in canon 1108.

The requirement concerns the placing of a condition "de futuro" on marriage consent, contained in canon 1102 §1: "Matrimonium sub condicione de futuro valide contrahi nequit." The nature of this norm – whether it is of natural or ecclesiastical law – can be argued. Insofar as it is a significant change from the previous legislation, one can affirm that it is positive ecclesiastical law and non retroactive. However, the present norm is now in harmony with longstanding jurisprudence which has judged a condition "de futuro" to be contrary to the nature of marriage.

6. CONCLUSION

In conclusion, we have engaged in an exercise of integrating a few general norms of Book One of the Code with the norms of a specific substantive legislation, marriage. We began with an analysis of the canons "De actibus iuridicis" in order to identify the essential elements of juridical acts and the possible causes of invalidity. For each of those elements – the capacity of the person to posit the act, the constitutive elements of the act itself, and the formalities and requirements imposed by law for validity – we sought to examine how marriage can be understood as a juridical act, in the light of the general norms. The marriage consent, lawfully manifested between persons qualified by law, brings marriage into being. No human power is able to supply this consent.

Thank you very much.

LIVING VALUES.
THE CONSTITUTION FOR EUROPE AND
THE LAW ON RELIGION

GERHARD ROBBERS

I. SUMMING UP THE RELIGIOUS EXPERIENCE

The Constitution for Europe is a true constitution. It is based in an international treaty, but this does not take away any of the substance of being constitutional law. Calling it a constitutional treaty is not wrong, but it draws the attention away from the impact a constitution can have on the integration of the European people. In history there are many examples for constitutions based in international agreements. The Germany of the 1815 German Federation is one example.

The very fact of a constitution is a highly important symbol for the integration of Europe. Constitutions entail the basics of a specific legal system. Constitutions lay down the structure by which a society decides to develop its legal life. The Constitution for Europe fulfills all these requirements. It also calls itself a constitution, not merely a constitutional treaty. It thus makes the explicit statement to be a constitution in its own right. The normative power of the language of the constitution does make it a constitution. The Constitution for Europe covers all areas of law that constitutions traditionally cover. So it does with the realm of religion.

In its Preamble the Constitution for Europe already refers to religion. In its very beginning the constitution says:
"Drawing inspiration from the cultural, religious and humanist inheritance of Europe, from which have developed the universal values of the inviolable and inalienable rights of the human person, freedom, democracy, equality and the rule of law".[1]

The constitution provides for religious freedom and religious non-discrimination. It refers to religious education, religious diversity, and religious rites. It establishes a dynamic relationship of the Union with

---

[1] Preamble, Treaty establishing a Constitution for Europe, Conference of the representatives of the governments of the Member States 13.10.2004 – CIG 87/1/04.

churches and religious communities, thus respecting religion in its institutional existence.

There are new provisions about religion in the Constitution for Europe
such as the religious reference in the Preamble and the founding of an
open and transparent and regular dialogue with the churches. There are
traditional and familiar provisions such as religious non-discrimination.
There are also young yet familiar guarantees such as the Union's respect
for the status of churches and religious communities under Member
States' law – this today is a non-directly binding declaration attached to
the Final Act of the Treaty of Amsterdam. There are further long familiar provisions such as the guarantee for freedom of religion and belief,
again pre-constitutionally existing as non-directly binding law in the
European Charter of Fundamental Rights, as binding law in the treaty's
reference to the European Convention of Human Rights and in the common constitutional traditions of the Member States.

Now, with the Constitution for Europe, this corpus of constitution-like
law on religion is turning into a true codex. Respecting regional traditions, developing a dialogue, fostering freedom of religion – all this will
be truly and directly binding law. From helpful and certainly important
arguments as some of those provisions are, now these legal statements
turn into reliable anchors of binding law. The present patchwork of binding and non-binding, direct and indirect legal references on religion now
will form a structured system of law.

The Constitution for Europe creates a normative system in which all
provisions basically share the same rank and value. Within the unity of
the constitution the provisions of religion have no lesser relevance than
those on economy or traffic. Within the Constitution for Europe religion
and the churches have the chance to contribute with their knowledge,
with their wisdom, with their social vigour, and with their all encompass-
ing message to a peaceful society. The Constitution for Europe adds up to
a sum the religious experiences and expectations of the Member States.

II. THE RELIGIOUS INHERITANCE OF EUROPE

In the Constitution for Europe, there is no reference to God. There is
no reference to Christianity. Is there no reference to God? Is there no
reference to Christianity in the Constitution for Europe?

Turning to the Preamble: The Constitution for Europe draws inspiration
from the religious inheritance of Europe. Alike Christian iconography,

religion stands in the middle between culture and humanism, marking the centre, the most important place for the most important idea. One should not underestimate these symbols: Time and again the number three appears as it does with the trias cultural, religious and humanist; in the flag of the European Union the twelve stars represent a number of deep symbolic impact; the anthym of the European Union rejoices with the divine, God's spark, in its original text. Drawing inspiration from the religious inheritance – these words figure in the very first sentence of the Preamble, in the first sentence of the constitution as such. This place marks the predominant importance of this inheritance.

It is the inheritance of Europe, not just any religious inheritance that constitutes the source of inspiration. This connection draws the attention to the facts of history. Religious diversity certainly is respected in Article II-82. All religions have their proper place. This notwithstanding, it just is a matter of fact that it is Christianity that has coined Europe's religious inheritance. The Preamble refers implicitly but visibly to Christianity – from which the constitution draws inspiration. It is the religious inheritance of Europe that there is one personal God and not many or none. Judaism, Greek and Roman, Egyptian, and many other influences of religious history have contributed and have their place in the inheritance of Europe. Islam has contributed more to European thought than often is remembered. Avicenna and Averroe, the Tales of A Thousand and One Night, Arabic digits and Muslim mathematics – Europe can and Europe should remember more what it has in common with other cultures in an ever closer world and it should less stress the differences that are obvious. It is the European idea of "United in diversity" that calls for the respect of the difference. The very European idea is: the peace of religions.

The Preamble goes on with relating to facts. It reminds all people of the fact that from the religious inheritance of Europe have developed the universal values of the inviolable and inalienable rights of the human person, freedom, democracy, equality and the rule of law. The constitution owes and pays reverence to the religious roots. It knows where it comes from.

However, there is more than just the facts in these first sentences of the constitution; the sentence has normative force. Only those religious ideas count that in fact have born all those positive ideas as the rights of the human person, freedom, democracy, equality and the rule of law. Others that have not are disregarded. One just has to turn back to history to see that Christianity is the core of this development.

There is no reference to the name of God. There is no reference to the word Christianity. However, the basics are there. It is much more important that the values are present than the words. Perhaps, in an economised world it may be more important for many to look at what is written advertising on the packing and not to care about the contents. Religion should know better: the truth comes from within. Religion should not remain blind and deaf because at first sight the name is not there, religion should see the message enshrined in the constitution.

III. LIVING VALUES

Religious values are present throughout the constitution. The Constitution for Europe is a constitution of living values. The Constitution for Europe protects explicitly family and marriage. It guarantees the right to religious education. The constitution makes solidarity a principle compulsory for and in all Member States. Subsidiarity with its roots in Christian teaching is a principle of the Union today. And is not the right to asylum based in the right to church asylum – ancient religious right?

One can and one should also look closer: Human dignity is enshrined in the Union's values in Article I-2. Human dignity is one of the core principles and guarantees of the European Charter of Fundamental Rights. The constitution promotes this Charter into binding European Union law. Human dignity is a key concept of Christianity. It is based in the idea of every human being "being created an image of God. The inviolability of human dignity is a prescriptive norm to all European Union authorities. As a basic value it pervades through all European Union law as binding norm. Human dignity is inviolable. So says Article II-61: human dignity in fact is inviolable, may there come what may, may the individual fail and do wrong the worst possible. Regardless of one's achievements or failures, regardless of talents or disabilities of any performance: human dignity is inviolable. This expresses the fact of inviolability of human dignity based in the theology of St. Paul.

The constitutional guarantee of equality that is enshrined throughout the constitution has a firm basis in the religious idea of equality of everyone before God. Freedom as a principle and as a right cannot be understood without the very idea of everybody's freedom before God. "The truth will make thou free" is a word of immense power well into modern law. Freedom of religion is a basically religious idea found in Thomas Aquinas, teaching respect also for the erring conscience, found in the Second Vatican Council, found in the idea that true belief must be free belief; by force there is no belief, by force there is only obedience.

One must not forget all the errors of religion in history. Religious ideas and institutions throughout history have also fought and failed against these ideas of human dignity, human rights and human freedoms. However, through all the blood and suffering it were these religious ideas that were held and prevailed also against those who misunderstood, misinterpreted or misused their own religion. We have modern examples of this today.

Canon law has been tremendously important to hand over Roman legal structures into modern Europe. Canon law has developed norms to protect every individual. Audiatur et altera pars or the procedural principle of inquisition – that means to find the facts by the court itself – prevails in many legal systems until today. Data protection has a predecessor in the idea of the confessional secret. It is the rule of law that canon law prepares. The list of legal achievements by canon law as an avantgarde of modern legal thinking is long and can be prolonged immensely.

Religion has contributed decisive institutions to democracy. Synods can be seen as predecessors of parliaments. Hierarchical ecclesiastical structures give a forecast to the hierarchical structures of democratic rule. Again, one must not forget all the setbacks, all the opposition by religious believers and institutions. It is, however, the idea that counts. All these ideas live in contemporary religious teaching of the churches. Human rights in the Codex Iuris Canonici or in the constitutions of protestant churches upkeep and deepen this tradition. The contribution of the churches to the democratic development based in human rights of the European Union is evident. And it is all there in the Constitution for Europe.

IV. THE NEW MEANING OF RELIGIOUS FREEDOM

Freedom of religion gains a new meaning. Religious freedom has been framed in Article II-70 after the religious freedom guarantee in Article 9 of the European Convention of Human Rights. It thus keeps in line with tradition, it reiterates and reinforces a long standing, basic guarantee. By not changing the words it emphasizes the basic importance of religious freedom.

Yet, the religious freedom clause in the Constitution for Europe carries a new meaning. Within the Charter of Fundamental Rights religious freedom holds a unique position. Other rights and freedoms guaranteed are limited by the general limitation clause in Article II-112 Sec. 1. Religious freedom does not. Article II-112 Sec. 3 says that insofar as this Charter contains rights which correspond to rights guaranteed by the European Convention of Human Rights, the meaning and the scope of these rights shall be the same as those laid down by the said convention. This does apply to the religious freedom clause. Because it has the same wording as the religious freedom clause in the European Convention of Human Rights, it is the limitation clause of Article 9 Sec. 2 ECHR that applies also to the provision in the European Charter of Fundamental Rights. These limits are not as strict as those provided for in the European Charter. This gives religious freedom in the Constitution for Europe a broader sense than other rights and freedoms have. Religious freedom, in some way, is elevated.

The same words in a different constitution do not mean the same. Not everything that has been said and has been decided in relation to religious freedom in the European Convention of Human Rights can also be said for religious freedom in the Constitution for Europe. Certainly, much can be just copied. However, within the Constitution for Europe, religious freedom finds itself in a different system, in different political perspectives, in different legal tasks. The Constitution for Europe is a constitution; the European Convention of Human Rights is an international treaty. Their raison d'être is different.

Religious freedom within the framework of the Constitution for Europe meets with other norms and aims. The reason why religious freedom must be guaranteed will remain highly individual, spiritual, and internal for every human being. Within the European Union further reasons become relevant. Freedom of religion contributes to peace and understanding. It takes pressure from the individual and from groups. Within the European Union religious freedom in its collective and corporative meaning gains importance. Europe unites by states, by nations, by cultures. Europe also unites by religions, churches, and religious communities. Whereas in the United States the highly individualistic approach to religious freedom is a key to integrating the diverse community, in Europe it is the community approach. Europe does not integrate by individual immigrants leaving behind their home countries. Europe unites not leaving anything behind, but in the respect of the other nations with all their history, experiences, and religious affiliations. Religion has been over centuries the key in forming European nations. Religion is now a key in forming the European Union. Orthodox churches in symphonia or at least close conjunction with the national governments will be decisive for the success of integrating such countries into the European Union. Established, state or peoples' churches in many countries have dominant influence, as have churches with overwhelming majority impact in some. Religious freedom for the institutions as such will be a key to forming a European public. Churches and religious communities are partners of politics, often times critical partners, but partners. Religious freedom in Europe has a function in forming a unied Europe. It will be one of the major challenges for the future to strengthen the community element also in European Islam. It is a major challenge to make Islam a partner of Europe.

The more it is religious non-discrimination that becomes relevant. There is a balance to be found between group rights and individual rights, a balance also for new groups to come into traditional settings. The Constitution for Europe stresses the importance of religious equality by anchoring it even twice: Article II-81 and Article III-118. More than individual religious freedom it will be religious equality that will form a centre of future debate.

V. THE IMPACT OF THE INSTITUTIONS

The Constitution for Europe shows awareness of the growing relevance of religion by strengthening the institutional structures of religion. The constitution thus acknowledges that the anarchical potential of religion needs institutional structures to counterbalance. The constitution brings the Church Declaration of Amsterdam into binding constitutional law.

The Union respects and does not prejudice the status under national law of churches and religious associations or communities in the Member States. So says Article I-52 Sec. 1 of the Constitution for Europe. It is the respect for the law of the Member States. This respect is paid to diversity and multitude of different state-church relationships within the European Union. Even within the Member States like in France, the United Kingdom or in Germany these relationships differ considerably within the countries themselves. The Union respects laïcité and neutrality, cooperation and established church systems. The Constitution for Europe establishes a principle of regionality in state-church relationships. This principle of regionality goes alongside with many other principles of religious freedom, tolerance, openness for religion, and non-discrimination.

Whoever should regret that in the Preamble there is no explicit, though implicit, reference to Christianity should note that the term church figures in Article I-52. Church is a genuinely Christian term, other religions do not have the term religion. The Constitution for Europe does make explicit reference to Christianity.

The provision is quite explicit, perhaps abundant in using the terms churches and religious associations or communities. This makes sure that all the various forms of legal personality, of legal existence and of social appearance of religious institutions within the Member States would be covered. It equally applies not only for the churches as such, but also for associations cultuelles or associations diocesaines as well as for other legal instruments religions make use of in France, it applies to churches and religious communities in the United Kingdom and their trusts, it applies to religiously oriented legal entities in Germany such as schools, hospitals or kindergartens, just to take examples.

The respect is for the Member States' law, not directly for the churches and religious communities. However, the European Union does take account of these entities. The Union refers positively to them.

Article I-52 Sec. 2 of the constitution makes equal reference to philosophical and non-confessional organisations. This is what in German constitutional law is called "Weltanschauungsgemeinschaften", communities of Weltanschauung. In a number of Member States of the European Union these communities for long enjoy the same status as churches and religious communities. This can be seen as a common constitutional tradition of the Member States. Although the wording of Section 2 does not include the words "and does not prejudice" the meaning of Section 2 and Section 1 in this respect is the same. The term "equally" refers to the whole sentence "respects and does not prejudice" in Section 1.

The provision prescribes how the European Union has to exercise its existing competencies. Whenever a power of the Union is touching the status of churches and the other relevant communities and organisations the Union must respect the status of these under national law. It has done so in the Council Directive establishing a general framework for equal treatment in employment and occupation[2] by which Member States may maintain national legislation respecting the ethos of institutions based on religion or believe as a relevant factor in the field of occupation.

---

[2] Council Directive 2000/78/EC of 27 November 2000, Official Journal L303, 02/12/2000 p. 0016-0022.

Article I-52 Sec. 1 and 2 are not exemptions from the competences of the Union. The provision does not take away any existing competences of the Union nor does it exclude any future Union competences in the field of religion if the Member States should so wish. The provision makes a statement on how the Union shall exercise its competences: respecting the status of the churches in the Member States.

Article I-52 is part of the unity of the Constitution for Europe. It has the same rank as other provisions such as freedom of religion or non-discrimination. As far as the Constitution for Europe applies the respect for the status under national law of churches and equivalent entities in the Member States does not allow to do away with freedom of religion or non-discrimination. If doubts should occur whether a specific provision in Member States' law is in line with religious freedom or non-discrimination relevant to Union law a proper balance must be found of the legal values protected in Article I-52 and in the other relevant provisions.

VI. DEVELOPING THE DIALOGUE

Section 3 of Article I-52 is a further step towards a genuine European Union law on religion. The Union shall maintain an open, transparent and regular dialogue with these churches and organisations. The sentence makes reference to the churches and organisations mentioned in the previous sections. These are churches and organisations that have a status under national law of the Member States.

It is the Union as such that has to maintain the dialogue. This is the first difference to Article I-47 according to which the institutions of the Union are obligated to maintain a similar dialogue with the organisations of civil society. Article I-52 is broader; the dialogue must be maintained not only by the institutions, but by any part of the Union.

The dialogue must be open. The dialogue must be positive and maintained in trust. No formal structures are required, but formal structures are possible if they are established in mutual agreement.

The dialogue must be transparent. Any religion interested must be brought into the position to be able to know where to go for information and dialogue. It should be clear with whom the Union is maintaining the dialogue. Transparency does not exclude trustful secrecy if necessary.

The dialogue must be regular. It must be more than once and occasional. How often meetings should take place is left to the needs of the concerned and the adequate resources they have.

What kind of meetings, negotiations, talks, e-mail exchanges or informations are preferable is not decided in the text. It can take the form of non-obliging conversation – the commission could meet on a more or less regular basis with representatives of churches for dinner. It could take the form of agreements non-formal or formal, of treaties or covenances.

The dialogue must be a dialogue. This is a mutual process that requires two active partners. With the fact of dialogue a further step is done to make churches and religious communities as well as non-confessional organisations partners of the Union. A Constitution for Europe establishes a cooperation concept, a partnership profile. The Union will be active in "maintaining" this dialogue, it must not be just passive and waiting.

The Union maintains the dialogue with the churches recognizing their identity. The Union does acknowledge that churches and equivalent organisations are something different from organisations of civil society. The organisations of civil society have their place in Article I-47. The specific identity of churches is already acknowledged by the fact that the Constitution for Europe attributes a special place in its text to churches distinct from the organisations of civil society. It is further stressed by the explicit recognition of their identity.

The provision recognizes the fact that churches are not a mere secular phenomenon. Implicitly, the Union also recognizes the dimension of the transcendental by recognizing the identity of those institutions that stand precisely representative for this sphere.

Recognizing their identity the Union respects the broad range of variety of churches and equivalent organisations. The Union is aware of the fact that each one of them requires in a specific way to have and to follow the truth. This prohibits to organize the dialogue in a way that forces these entities to find a consensus on one or several representatives or issues. Each one of these entities must be partner of the European Union in its own right.

By recognizing their identity the European Union can distinguish among these partners according to size, tradition or proximity to values spelled out in the first sentence of the Preamble.

Part of their identity also is the existence of churches as legal entities in their various specific forms. The European Union recognizes the Holy See as an entity of public international law by recognizing the identity of the Roman-Catholic Church. It acknowledges the existence of the Anglican Church as the established church of England or the Danish Lutheran Church as the peoples' church of Denmark. Respecting the Holy See as

an entity of public international law will also allow a concordat or concordatarian agreements between the European Union and the Roman-
Catholic Church. As a consequence of equal treatment covenantal agreements are therefore possible also with other churches and religious or
non-confessional communities. This possibility also springs from the
common constitutional traditions of the Member States as forming part
of the Union's law.

Recognizing their identity also and perhaps predominantly means the
respect for the needs of autonomy and self-determination of churches
and equivalent organisations. Such identity is formed especially and for-
mostly by adhering to one's own specific belief. Teaching, internal
structure, and the way such entities perform in society form the very
identity of these communities and fall within the range of self-determination. Certainly, there are limits to this self-determination. These spring
from the full range of provisions of the Constitution for Europe maintaining due regard to the identity of these communities. These limits
must not go further than the limits for religious freedom guaranteed in
Article II-70; self-determination of churches also is guaranteed by the
freedom of religion.

The European Union recognizes the specific contribution of these
churches and organisations. The European Union does acknowledge the
full range of contributions that churches do make to the life of and
within the European Union. It is thus recognized that churches perform
the full range of activities according to their own teaching. It is not only
the teaching in words as such – important enough – but also and equally
important the activity according to this teaching, their teaching by activity. The Union thus recognizes that churches care for the poor and those
in need, that they run hospitals and homes, schools and universities, that
they have to care for their subsistence. Also, the Union recognized their
contributions onto the democratic life of the Union, their share in public
communication, their part in forming a European public. All this is part
of church activity and their specific contribution.

This contribution is a specific one. This also places these churches
and organizations beyond mere organizations of civil society.

VII. THE RANGE OF RESPECTING THE RELIGIOUS

The freedom to found educational establishments with religious ethos
is guaranteed in Article II-74. Churches can run schools, universities,

seminaries and the like. Article I-52 obligates the Union to respect the specific basis and needs of these institutions. This guarantee is imbedded within the due respect for democratic principles and the national laws governing the exercise of this freedom. The latter refers to what is already stated in Article I-52 Sec. 1 and 2. The due respect for democratic principles furthermore is a necessary and legitimate barrier against those religious or non-confessional communities that preach anti-democratic or non-democratic and totalitarian ideas. This is well in line with the common constitutional traditions of the Member States.

Parents have the right to ensure the education and teaching of their children in conformity with their religious convictions. Thus, some kind of religious instruction in the religion of the child must be adequately possible.

Religious diversity is respected by the Union (Article II-82). This adds to the Union's respect for the Member States law on religion, it adds to the recognition of the identity of the manifold churches, religious and non-confessional organizations. It adds to the guarantee of freedom of religion and belief. Article II-82 holds all these principles in a nutshell. Again, there is the trias of respected phenomena, the religion in the middle, the reverence also made to the beauty of law, to legal aesthetics.

The provision is a cornerstone of religious tolerance. It is an expression of the very identity of the European Union with its motto "United in diversity".

Article III-121 specifies one aspect of this diversity: The respect to religious rites within the Union's regard to animal's welfare. Ritual slaughter to produce halal or kosher meat, but also other possible rites involving animals find their due respect, here. This cannot mean a disregard of the animal's welfare whenever religion so commands. It means to harmonize relevant and legitimate needs and to especially develop the aspect of animal welfare that is a very basis of ritual slaughter.

VIII. EQUALITY AND DIVERSITY

Religious equality is particularly stressed by the Constitution for Europe in Article II-81 and Article III-118, but also right across the constitution. Equality is meant when Article II-70 guarantees to "everyone" the right to freedom of religion, or when the identity and the specific contribution of all the churches and organizations referring to Article I-52 find themselves recognized.

Non-discrimination prohibits unequal treatment without valid reasons. Equal treatment does not mean identical treatment. In regard to the constitutional side of religious freedom this is already being expressed in the recognition of the identity of religious constitutions and in the respect for religious diversity. It is the very motto of the Union "United in diversity" that coins the understanding of equality and non-discrimination within the Constitution for Europe. It so matches with the common constitutional traditions of the Member States and international instruments. Equality within non-discrimination means to treat equal what is equal and to treat unequal what is unequal according to the amount of inequality. Whenever there are valid reasons the Union can and must distinguish. There is no discrimination when there is a valid reason for different treatment. Valid reasons for different treatment are constituted by the values of the European Union laid down in its constitution.

IX. BEING OPEN FOR RELIGION

In interpreting the Constitution for Europe the fact of numerous official languages must be taken into account. In all of the now 20 official languages the constitution has the same relevance and legally binding force. All texts in all the official languages are equally valid. This opens a wide range of interpretation. The meaning of the words have different ranges and perspectives in different languages. All these broad meanings have to be brought together. This means that it is not possible in the interpretation of European Union law to stick to the meaning of the words in just one of the official languages. Sometimes this phenomenon has given rise to conscious political playing with words. In the time of framing the Preamble of the European Charter of Fundamental Rights it was not possible to find a consensus on the topic of religious inheritance. Here, in the very wording of constitutional law the French text "patrimoine spirituel" or the English text "spiritual heritage" reads in its German official text "geistig-religiöses Erbe". This brings the religious demand into the text by using the margins of meaning in languages. This compromise left it open to forthcoming interpretation to decide on the reference to religion.

It is one of the major steps from the Charter of Fundamental Rights to the Constitution for Europe that in the Preamble of the Constitution a consensus has been found to openly rely on religion in all official languages and for all Member States. This is an important step also for the development of the European identity.

The specific and manifold provisions concerning religion in the Constitution for Europe constitute basic principles underlying the Union's law on religion: These principles are freedom of religion, tolerance, religious equality, regionality, respect for diversity, and openness for religion.

PERSONALIA

MICHAEL HILBERT, S.J., was born in New York (U.S.A.) in 1951. After receiving his B.A. in International Relations from Colgate University in 1973, he entered the Society of Jesus (Jesuits). Philosophy studies were done at Fordham University, and Chinese Language studies at Fu Jen University in Taipei, Taiwan. He received his STB, JCL, and JCD (cum specializatione in iurisprudentia) from the Pontifical Gregorian University, where he has been on the canon law faculty since 1991, and Dean of the Faculty since September, 2004. From 2000 to 2004 he was Vice Rector for Academic Affairs of the University. He is a judge on the Appellate Tribunal for the Vicariate of Rome and member of the Editorial Board of *Communicationes*. From 1995 to 2000 he was Visiting Professor at the Catholic University in Budapest. His memberships include the *Consociatio Internationalis Studio Iuris Canonici Promovendo*, the *Canon Law Society of America*, and the *Canon Law Society of Great Britain and Ireland*.

GERHARD ROBBERS was born in Bonn in 1950. He received his doctoral degree in Law in 1978 and obtained his final law degree in 1980 in Freiburg. From 1981-1984 he served as Law Clerk to the President of the German Federal Constitutional Court. In 1986 he obtained his habilitation in Law. From 1988 to 1989 he was Professor of Law at the University of Heidelberg. Since 1989 he is Professor for Public Law at the University of Trier. He is Director of the Institute for European Constitutional Law and Director of the Institute for Legal Policy. He serves as judge at the Administrative Court of Appeals Rhineland-Palatine. In 2003-2004 he was president of the *European Consortium of Church and State Research*, of which he is a member. He is also member of the *Advisory Council for Freedom of Religion* at ODIHR/OSCE. His main areas of work are the law on religion, constitutional law and international public law. He is advisor to several national governments and international organizations. Selection of Publications: *An Introduction to German Law*, 3rd edition 2003 (also in German: 3rd ed. 2002); *State and Church in the European Union* (ed.), 1997 (also in German, French, Italian, Spanish, Hungarian and Czech). Further publications in public law, civil ecclesiastical law, legal philosophy, constitutional history, and European Union law.

RIK TORFS was born in Turnhout (Belgium) in 1956. He studied law (lic. iur., 1979; lic. not., 1980) and canon law (J.C.D., 1987) at the Katholieke Universiteit Leuven. After one year of teaching at Utrecht University (The Netherlands), he became professor at the Faculty of Canon Law (K.U. Leuven) in 1988. He was dean of the Faculty of Canon Law between 1994 and 2003. Since 2000, he is visiting professor at the University of Stellenbosch (South Africa). In 2003, he was president of the *European Consortium for State-Church Research* of which he is still a member. He is also member of the redaction committee of the *Revue de droit canonique* (Strasbourg), member of the board of the *International Academy for Freedom of Religion and Belief* (Washington) and editor of the *European Journal for Church and State Research* (Leuven).

PUBLICATIES / PUBLICATIONS
MSGR. W. ONCLIN CHAIR

Editors RIK TORFS & KURT MARTENS

Canon Law and Marriage. Monsignor W. Onclin Chair 1995, Leuven, Peeters, 1995, 36 p.

R. TORFS, *The Faculty of Canon Law of K.U. Leuven in 1995*, 5-9.
C. BURKE, *Renewal, Personalism and Law*, 11-21.
R.G.W. HUYSMANS, *Enforcement and Deregulation in Canon Law*, 23-36.

A Swing of the Pendulum. Canon Law in Modern Society. Monsignor W. Onclin Chair 1996, Leuven, Peeters, 1996, 64 p.

R. TORFS, *Une messe est possible. Over de nabijheid van Kerk en geloof*, 7-11.
R. TORFS, *'Une messe est possible'. A Challenge for Canon Law*, 13-17.
J.M. SERRANO RUIZ, *Acerca del carácter personal del matrimonio: digresiones y retornos*, 19-31.
J.M. SERRANO RUIZ, *The Personal Character of Marriage. A Swing of the Pendulum*, 33-45.
F.G. MORRISEY, *Catholic Identity of Healthcare Institutions in a Time of Change*, 47-64.

In Diversitate Unitas. Monsignor W. Onclin Chair 1997, Leuven, Peeters, 1997, 72 p.

R. TORFS, *Pro Pontifice et Rege*, 7-13.
R. TORFS, *Pro Pontifice et Rege*, 15-22.
H. PREE, *The Divine and the Human of the Ius Divinum*, 23-41.
J.H. PROVOST, *Temporary Replacements or New Forms of Ministry: Lay Persons with Pastoral Care of Parishes*, 43-70.

Bridging Past and Future. Monsignor W. Onclin Revisited. Monsignor W. Onclin Chair 1998, Leuven, Peeters, 1998, 87 p.

P. CARD. LAGHI, *Message*, 7-9.
R. TORFS, *Kerkelijk recht in de branding. Terug naar monseigneur W. Onclin*, 11-20.
R. TORFS, *Canon Law in the Balance. Monsignor W. Onclin Revisited*, 21-31.

L. Örsy, *In the Service of the Holy Spirit: the Ecclesial Vocation of the Canon Lawyers*, 33-53.
P. Coertzen, *Protection of Rights in the Church. A Reformed Perspective*, 55-87.

Church and State. Changing Paradigms. Monsignor W. Onclin Chair 1999, Leuven, Peeters, 1999, 72 p.

R. Torfs, *Crisis in het kerkelijk recht*, 7-17.
R. Torfs, *Crisis in Canon Law*, 19-29.
C. Migliore, *Ways and Means of the International Activity of the Holy See*, 31-42.
J.E. Wood, Jr., *The Role of Religion in the Advancement of Religious Human Rights*, 43-69.

Canon Law and Realism. Monsignor W. Onclin Chair 2000, Leuven, Peeters, 2000, 92 p.

R. Torfs, *De advocaat in de kerk, of de avonturen van een vreemdeling in het paradijs*, 7-28.
R. Torfs, *The Advocate in the Church. Source of Conflict or Conflict Solver*, 29-49.
J.P. Beal, *At the Crossroads of Two Laws. Some Reflections on the Influence of Secular Law on the Church's Response to Clergy Sexual Abuse in the United States*, 51-74.
Ch.K. Papastathis, *Unity Among the Orthodox Churches. From the Theological Approach to the Historical Realities*, 75-88.

Canon Law Between Interpretation and Imagination. Monsignor W. Onclin Chair 2001, Leuven, Peeters, 2001, 88 p.

J. Coriden, *Necessary Canonical Reform: Urgent Issues for the Future*, 7-25.
R. Pagé, *Full Time Lay Pastoral Ministers and Diocesan Governance*, 27-40.
R. Torfs, *Kerkelijke rechtbanken* secundum *en* praeter legem, 41-61.
R. Torfs, *Church Tribunals* secundum *and* praeter legem, 63-84.

Many Cultures, Many Faces. Monsignor W. Onclin Chair 2002, Leuven, Peeters, 2002, 112 p.

R. Torfs, *Dwarsverbindingen*, 7-17.
R. Torfs, *Cross-connections*, 19-29.

J.R. TRETERA, *Systems of Relations Between the State and Churches in General (Systems of State Ecclesiastical Law) and Their Occurence in the Czech Lands in Particular*, 31-56.
A. MENDONÇA, Bonum Coniugum *from a Socio-Cultural Perspective*, 57-108.

Canon Law, Consultation and Consolation. Monsignor W. Onclin Chair 2003, Leuven, Peeters, 2003, 163 p.

R. TORFS, *De opleiding kerkelijk recht na de Romeinse hervorming*. Per aspera ad astra*?*, 7-24.
R. TORFS, *The Roman Reform of the Canon Law Programme*. Per aspera ad astra*?*, 25-41.
T.J. GREEN, *The Legislative Competency of the Episcopal Conference: Present Situation and Future Possibilities*, 43-98.
I.C. IBAN, *Concordates in the European Union: a Relic from the Past or a Valid Instrument for the XXI Century?*, 99-157.

Canonical Testament. Monsignor W. Onclin Chair 2004, Leuven, Peeters, 2004, 77 p.

R. TORFS, *Tien jaar Monsignor W. Onclin Chair. Tussenbericht of testament?*, 7-14.
R. TORFS, *Ten Years Monsignor W. Onclin Chair. An Interim Report or a Testament?*, 15-22.
B. DE GAAY FORTMAN, *Quod omnes tangit*, 23-43.
J.D. VAN DER VYVER, *Contributions of the Holy See to the Refinement of the Rome Statute of the Internatioal Criminal Court*, 45-72.

PRINTED ON PERMANENT PAPER • IMPRIME SUR PAPIER PERMANENT • GEDRUKT OP DUURZAAM PAPIER - ISO 9706

N.V. PEETERS S.A., WAROTSTRAAT 50, B-3020 HERENT